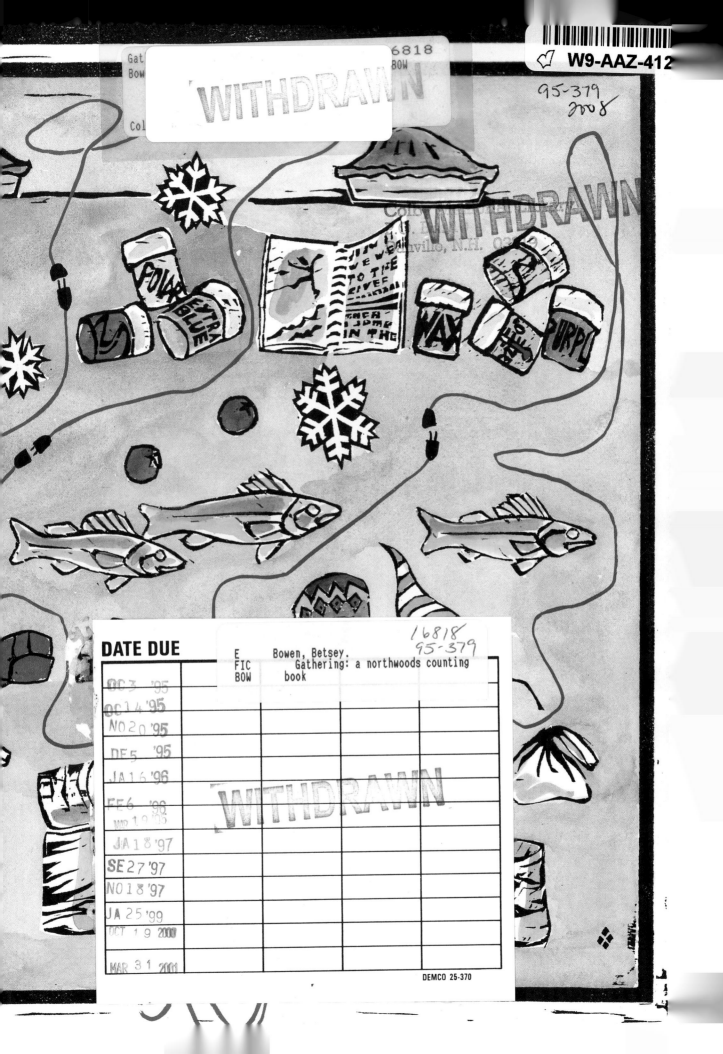

Gathering

Gathering

A NORTHWOODS COUNTING BOOK

Betsy Bowen

Little, Brown and Company
Boston   New York   Toronto   London

Zero degrees

It's springtime in the northwoods. Winter seems a long way off. But in only a few months, the temperature will be down to zero, the lakes frozen, the flowers and leaves gone, and the bears and skunks asleep in their dens. So all through the warm, bright days of summer and the crisp, clear days of fall, we'll gather food and firewood and memories to be ready for the white snow and the cold, dark nights when they come.

MAY

One seed

In late May, we start planting. Each vegetable in the garden starts with just one seed. It takes a long time to tend and grow the food we'll need to last through the winter: tomatoes and beans for canning, plus piles of carrots, potatoes, rutabagas, and squash. In February, when we eat the vegetables we've grown, they will have the fresh taste of summer and they will smell like the earth.

1

MAY

Two rhubarb pies

Every year the bright red rhubarb stalks, with their big curled leaves, come up by themselves. We never have to replant. By June the plants are huge. Sometimes when we go to pick, we spot toads living in the dark, cool spaces under the leaves. There's so much rhubarb, we make two pies right away, then put the extra in the freezer to make into jam and cakes and more pies during the winter.

2

JUNE

Three summer memories

Summer is the time to let loose in the northwoods. It is the shortest of all the seasons, and we need to collect lots of warm memories to make it through the long, cold winter. By July we already have three especially good ones tucked away: floating along in the canoes under shooting stars, jumping off the cliff into the river, and catching a whole jarful of blinking fireflies.

3

JULY

Four bears

The animals here spend the warm months preparing for winter, too. Bears get ready by fattening up on berries and plants and grubs. We see four of them one afternoon, a mother and three cubs, eating raspberries in the woods. They have to eat now, because their food will be gone when the snow comes, and the bears must be fat enough to keep their big bodies warm during their winter sleep.

4

JULY

Five blueberries

Five blueberries isn't many to put away for winter, but that's all the littlest helper has in his tub because he keeps eating them — they're so ripe and sweet and warm from the sun. We'll put most of the berries in the freezer for later — to make into pancakes and muffins and pies. Some we make into jam with the rhubarb, and then we call it *bluebarb*. On snowy mornings, we'll pack frozen berries in our lunches; by noontime they are thawed and ready to eat. Yum!

5

AUGUST

Six bags of wild rice

When the wild rice ripens in September, we drop everything and go. We paddle to the marshy place in the lake where it grows, and whack it with sticks so the seeds fall into the bottom of the empty canoe. Later, we'll take the grain to be parched. We're hoping for six bags full, enough to cook for special dinners when visitors come, and some extra for hot, steaming winter soup. Wild rice is called *mahnomin* by the Ojibwe people here. They honor it as a gift to them from the Creator.

6

SEPTEMBER

Seven walleyes

On the last fishing trip of the season, we catch seven walleyes. The biggest weighs five pounds, a nice one to save in the freezer for Thanksgiving. We don't get any mosquito bites this trip; the chilly fall air has driven away the bugs. A few orange maple leaves are floating on the lake as we reel in. Time to put away the boat until next spring.

7

MN85385EY

SEPTEMBER

Eight
cords of
wood

On a blue-sky day in fall, our firewood arrives — eight cords of birch logs, enough to last this year and next. To make sure the chimney will be safe all season, the chimney sweep comes to clean it in his tall stovepipe hat. The wood burning in the warm winter stove will keep away the cold.

8

OCTOBER

Nine extension cords

The first snow turned the ground white for a few hours today. With the colder temperatures, the truck is a little slow to start, and we know that when the thermometer drops below zero, it won't start at all unless we plug it in. So we lay out nine extension cords end to end, to reach all the way from the house down the path to the truck. To help us see where to walk in the winter dark, we hang Christmas lights in the trees along the way. When a fresh snowfall covers them up, the snow will glow pink and blue and yellow.

OCTOBER

Ten skis

After we pull out all of the winter hats, mittens, coats, and boots, then find the snow shovels and fix the sleds, the last thing to get ready is our skis, all ten of them. We wax the bottoms and check to see who has grown out of last year's pair; we'll take the ones that are too short to the ski swap to trade. With the leaves off the trees now, we can see a long way through the woods. Soon the bigger snowfalls will come, and we'll have enough snow to ski on the trails back there.

10

NOVEMBER

Eleven friends

The season of chores is over now, so eleven good friends come for a feast. We gather around the table to eat garden beans and squash, stuffed walleye, wild rice, and blueberry pie for dessert. Someone saw a woolly-bear caterpillar today with a wide yellow stripe — that means a hard winter for sure. But we can't wait to ski, skate, and fish through the ice. We're ready now — let winter come!

11

NOVEMBER

Twelve inches

This morning, snowflakes started falling fast and thick from the soft gray sky. The buses took all the kids home early from school. So far the snow is twelve inches deep. Tomorrow we'll be able to ski!

12

DECEMBER

All day long

. . . we ski on the fresh snow; we find our familiar trails and discover some new ones, too. Tonight we'll gather around the fire to thaw our feet and drink hot cider. We're settled in for winter now.

Before long, we'll count the days until spring.

In honor of teachers,
enthusiastic and caring,
in particular,
Miss Glixon,
who taught me
to measure
the sun passing across the floor
through the seasons
of fourth grade.

First Edition

Library of Congress Cataloging-in-Publication Data
Bowen, Betsy.
   Gathering: a northwoods counting book /
Betsy Bowen.
      p.   cm.
   ISBN 0-316-10371-3
   1. Counting — Juvenile literature. 2. Natural
history — Minnesota — Juvenile literature.
3. Seasons — Minnesota — Juvenile literature.
[1. Natural history — Minnesota. 2. Country life —
Minnesota. 3. Seasons. 4. Counting.] I. Title.
QA113.B683   1995
513.2´11 — dc20
[E]   94-34491

10 9 8 7 6 5 4 3 2 1

NIL

Published simultaneously in Canada by
Little, Brown & Company (Canada) Limited

Printed in Italy

The pictures in this book are woodblock prints, made
by carving the design and the big letters, backwards,
into a flat block of pine, rolling black ink onto the
block, and then printing on a Vandercook No. 4 letter-
press housed at the Historic Grand Marais Art Colony.
The colors are then painted on each print.